FIX IT QUICK

COOKING *for* KIDS

Publications International, Ltd.

Favorite Brand Name Recipes at www.fbnr.com

Recipe Development: Maiko Miyamoto, Alison Reich and Marcia Kay Stanley, M.S., R.D.

Photography on pages 11, 15, 43, 63, 75, 87, 89, 95, 97, 101 and 105 by Maes Studio.

Photography on pages 5, 19, 21, 25, 27, 49, 51, 55, 61, 67, 77, 81, 83, 85, 93, 99, 109, 111, 115 and 117 by Proffitt Photography, Chicago.

Pictured on the front cover *(clockwise from top left):* Spotted Butterfly Sandwich *(page 28),* Chocolate Panini Bites *(page 64),* Cheesy Potato Head *(page 96)* and Corny Face *(page 32).*

Pictured on the back cover: Peanutty Crispy Dessert Cups *(page 108).*

ISBN-13: 978-1-4127-2733-4
ISBN-10: 1-4127-2733-2

Library of Congress Control Number: 2007936266

Manufactured in China.

8 7 6 5 4 3 2 1

Microwave Cooking: Microwave ovens vary in wattage. Use the cooking times as guidelines and check for doneness before adding more time.

Preparation/Cooking Times: Preparation times are based on the approximate amount of time required to assemble the recipe before cooking, baking, chilling or serving. These times include preparation steps such as measuring, chopping and mixing. The fact that some preparations and cooking can be done simultaneously is taken into account. Preparation of optional ingredients and serving suggestions is not included.

table of contents

rise & shine

bacon & egg cups

12 slices bacon, cut crosswise into thirds
6 eggs *or* **1½ cups egg substitute**
½ cup half-and-half
½ cup diced bell peppers (red, green or a combination)
½ cup shredded pepper jack cheese
¼ teaspoon salt
¼ teaspoon black pepper

1. Preheat oven to 350°F. Lightly spray 12 standard (2½-inch) muffin cups with nonstick cooking spray.

2. Arrange bacon slices flat in single layer on plate lined with paper towel. Do not overlap. Top with additional sheets of paper towel and microwave on HIGH 2 to 3 minutes or until cooked yet pliable. Place 3 bacon slices in each prepared muffin cup, overlapping in bottom of cup.

3. Beat eggs, half-and-half, bell peppers, cheese, salt and black pepper in medium bowl until well blended. Fill each muffin cup with ¼ cup egg mixture. Bake 20 to 25 minutes or until eggs are set in center. Run knife around edge of each cup before removing from pan.   *Makes 12 servings*

Tip: To save time, look for mixed diced bell peppers in the produce section of the grocery store.

bacon & egg cups

fruity breakfast bars

1 package (about 16 ounces) refrigerated oatmeal raisin cookie dough
⅓ cup uncooked old-fashioned oats
1 egg
2 tablespoons honey
⅓ cup chopped dried apricots or mango
⅓ cup dried cranberries
⅓ cup dried cherries
¼ cup sunflower kernels

1. Preheat oven to 350°F. Lightly grease 11×7-inch baking pan. Let dough stand at room temperature about 15 minutes.

2. Beat dough, oats, egg and honey in large bowl until well blended. Stir in dried fruit and sunflower kernels. Press dough evenly into prepared pan.

3. Bake 25 to 30 minutes or until edges are browned and toothpick inserted into center comes out clean. Cool completely in pan on wire rack.

Makes 16 bars

breakfast tacos

6 mini taco shells or 2 regular-sized taco shells
2 eggs
½ teaspoon taco seasoning mix
2 tablespoons shredded Cheddar cheese or cheese sauce
2 tablespoons mild salsa
2 tablespoons chopped fresh parsley
   Sliced green onion and shredded lettuce (optional)

1. Heat taco shells according to package directions; cool slightly. Meanwhile, beat eggs in small bowl until well blended. Spray small skillet with nonstick cooking spray; heat over medium-low heat. Pour eggs into skillet; cook, stirring often, until desired doneness. Sprinkle taco seasoning mix over eggs.

2. Spoon egg mixture into taco shells. Top each taco with 1 teaspoon *each* cheese, salsa and parsley. Sprinkle with green onion and lettuce.

Makes 2 servings

fruity breakfast bars

sunny day breakfast burritos

1 tablespoon butter
½ cup red or green bell pepper, chopped
2 green onions, sliced
6 eggs
2 tablespoons milk
¼ teaspoon salt
4 (7-inch) flour tortillas, warmed
½ cup shredded colby jack or Mexican cheese blend
½ cup salsa

1. Melt butter in medium skillet over medium heat. Add bell pepper and green onions; cook and stir about 3 minutes or until tender.

2. Beat eggs, milk and salt in medium bowl. Add egg mixture to skillet; reduce heat to low. Cook, stirring gently, until eggs are just set. (Eggs should be soft with no liquid remaining.)

3. Spoon one fourth of egg mixture down center of tortillas; top with cheese. Fold in sides to enclose filling. Serve with salsa.   *Makes 4 servings*

hawaiian breakfast pizza

2 teaspoons barbecue sauce or pineapple jam
1 English muffin, split in half and toasted
1 slice (1 ounce) smoked ham, diced
½ cup pineapple chunks
2 tablespoons shredded Cheddar cheese

1. Spread barbecue sauce over each muffin half; place on foil-lined toaster oven tray. Sprinkle ham and pineapple chunks over muffin halves; top with cheese.

2. Toast about 2 minutes or until cheese is melted.   *Makes 1 serving*

Note: To cook in a conventional oven, preheat oven to 400°F. Heat muffins on a foil-lined baking sheet about 5 minutes or until cheese is melted.

sunny day breakfast burrito

crunchy french toast sticks

6 (1-inch) slices Italian bread (about 3½- to 4-inches in diameter)
4 cups cornflakes, crushed
3 eggs
⅔ cup fat-free (skim) milk
1 tablespoon sugar
1 teaspoon ground cinnamon
1 teaspoon vanilla
¼ teaspoon ground nutmeg
1 (6-ounce) container low-fat vanilla yogurt
¼ cup maple syrup
Ground cinnamon (optional)

1. Preheat oven to 375°F. Lightly spray large baking sheet with nonstick cooking spray; set aside. Remove crusts from bread, if desired. Cut each bread slice into three strips. Place cereal on waxed paper.

2. Beat eggs, milk, sugar, 1 teaspoon cinnamon, vanilla and nutmeg in shallow bowl. Dip bread strips in egg mixture, turning to generously coat all sides. Roll in cereal, coating all sides. Place on prepared baking sheet.

3. Bake 25 to 28 minutes or until golden brown, turning sticks after 15 minutes.

4. Meanwhile, combine yogurt and syrup in small bowl. Sprinkle with additional cinnamon, if desired. Serve French toast sticks with yogurt mixture for dipping.   *Makes 6 servings*

Prep Time: 15 minutes
Bake Time: 25 minutes

crunchy french toast sticks

breakfast banana split

- **1 banana**
- **3 strawberries, sliced**
- **¼ cup fresh blueberries**
- **1 container (6 ounces) "fruit on the bottom" reduced-fat strawberry yogurt, mixed**
- **1 tablespoon granola**
- **1 maraschino cherry**

Peel banana; cut in half lengthwise. Place banana in serving dish and separate halves. Top with half of strawberries and blueberries. Gently spoon yogurt over berries. Top with remaining berries; sprinkle with granola. Garnish with cherry.   *Makes 1 serving*

strawberry cinnamon french toast

- **1 egg**
- **¼ cup fat-free (skim) milk**
- **½ teaspoon vanilla**
- **4 (1-inch-thick) slices French bread**
- **2 teaspoons sugar**
- **2 teaspoons butter, softened**
- **¼ teaspoon ground cinnamon**
- **1 cup sliced strawberries**

1. Preheat oven to 450°F. Spray nonstick baking sheet with nonstick cooking spray.

2. Beat egg, milk and vanilla in shallow dish. Dip bread slices in egg mixture until completely coated. Place on prepared baking sheet.

3. Bake 15 minutes or until golden brown, turning halfway through baking time. Meanwhile, combine sugar, butter and cinnamon in small bowl until well blended. Spread mixture evenly over French toast. Top with strawberries.   *Makes 4 servings*

Prep Time: 10 minutes
Bake Time: 15 minutes

breakfast banana split

ham & egg mini wafflewiches

1 egg, lightly beaten
2 teaspoons butter
8 frozen mini waffles (2 pieces, divided into individual waffles)
2 thin slices deli ham, cut in half
4 teaspoons shredded Cheddar cheese

1. Spray small skillet with cooking spray; heat over medium heat. Pour egg into skillet; cook and stir until set.

2. Spread one side of each waffle with butter. Place ham slice on unbuttered sides of 4 waffles. Top each with one fourth of cooked egg and 1 teaspoon cheese. Top with remaining 4 waffles, buttered sides up.

3. Heat medium skillet over medium heat. Cook sandwiches 3 to 4 minutes on each side, pressing with back of spatula until cheese melts and waffles are golden.   *Makes 2 servings*

triple berry blast

1 cup frozen mixed berries
1 cup soy milk*
½ cup sliced banana (about 1 small)
2 teaspoons honey

*Do not use vanilla-flavored soy milk because it will make the smoothie too sweet.

Combine berries, soy milk, banana and honey in blender; blend about 30 seconds or until smooth and thick. Serve immediately.   *Makes 2 servings*

Sugar-Dipped Glasses: For a festive look and taste, add sugar to the rim of your glasses. Wet the rim with water, juice or by running a lime or lemon along the rim. Then dip the glass in colored sugar.

ham & egg mini wafflewiches

peachy keen smoothies

2 cups frozen sliced peaches
1 container (6 ounces) reduced-fat peach yogurt
½ cup reduced-fat (2%) milk
¼ teaspoon vanilla

Combine peaches, yogurt, milk and vanilla in blender; blend until smooth. Pour into glasses.   *Makes 2 servings*

Prep Time: 5 minutes

apple & raisin oven pancake

1 large baking apple, cored and thinly sliced
⅓ cup golden raisins
2 tablespoons packed brown sugar
½ teaspoon ground cinnamon
4 eggs
⅔ cup milk
⅔ cup all-purpose flour
2 tablespoons butter, melted
Powdered sugar (optional)

1. Preheat oven to 350°F. Spray 9-inch pie plate with nonstick cooking spray.

2. Combine apple, raisins, brown sugar and cinnamon in medium bowl. Transfer to prepared pie plate. Bake, uncovered, 10 to 15 minutes or until apple begins to soften. Remove from oven. *Increase oven temperature to 450°F.*

3. Meanwhile, whisk eggs, milk, flour and butter in medium bowl until blended. Pour batter over apple mixture. Bake 15 minutes or until pancake is golden brown. Invert onto serving dish. Sprinkle with powdered sugar.
Makes 6 servings

peachy keen smoothies

french toast kabobs

8 slices French bread (about 1 inch thick, 2½ to 3 inches in diameter)
1 cup milk
2 eggs
3 tablespoons sugar
2 teaspoons vanilla
⅛ teaspoon salt
¾ cup tangerine juice or orange juice
¼ cup honey
2 teaspoons cornstarch
¼ teaspoon ground ginger or ground cinnamon
Powdered sugar
1 cup fresh raspberries

1. Preheat broiler. Generously grease broiler pan rack. Soak 4 (12-inch) wooden skewers in water while preparing bread.

2. Cut each bread slice in half crosswise. Beat milk, eggs, sugar, vanilla and salt in shallow dish until well blended. Place bread pieces in egg mixture. Let stand 5 minutes, turning to soak all sides.

3. Meanwhile, combine tangerine juice, honey, cornstarch and ginger in small saucepan; bring to a boil over medium-high heat, stirring constantly. Cook and stir 1 minute more. Set aside and keep warm.

4. Thread 4 pieces bread onto each skewer. Place on prepared broiler pan rack. Broil 4 to 5 inches from heat 5 to 7 minutes or until lightly browned. Turn skewers; broil 3 to 5 minutes more or until lightly browned.

5. Spoon juice mixture onto plates; top with French toast kabobs. Sprinkle with powdered sugar and raspberries. Serve immediately.

Makes 4 servings

Prep Time: 15 minutes
Cook Time: 8 minutes

french toast kabobs

puffy pancake

3 tablespoons melted butter, divided
½ cup reduced-fat (2%) milk
2 eggs
½ cup all-purpose flour
¼ teaspoon salt
2 bananas, sliced
1 cup sliced strawberries
2 tablespoons chocolate syrup
   Powdered sugar (optional)

1. Preheat oven to 400°F. Pour 2 tablespoons butter into 10-inch ovenproof skillet; brush onto side of pan.

2. Combine milk, eggs, flour, remaining 1 tablespoon butter and salt in medium bowl; whisk constantly 1 minute. Pour batter into prepared skillet.

3. Bake 20 to 22 minutes or until pancake is golden brown and puffed up side of pan. Remove from oven and immediately fill with fruit. Drizzle with chocolate syrup; sprinkle with powdered sugar.   *Makes 4 servings*

Tip: This pancake can also be prepared in a deep-dish pie pan.

dippy breakfast

1 container (6 ounces) fat-free vanilla yogurt
¼ cup peanut butter
2 tablespoons breakfast cereal
1 apple, cored and cut into wedges
1 orange, peeled and separated into segments
2 slices cinnamon or whole wheat bread, toasted

1. Combine yogurt and peanut butter in small bowl until blended. Divide mixture between 2 small bowls; sprinkle with cereal. Place bowls on serving plates.

2. Arrange fruit pieces around dip. Cut toast into strips and place half of strips on each plate.   *Makes 2 servings*

puffy pancake

quick breakfast sandwiches

2 turkey breakfast sausage patties
3 eggs
 Salt and black pepper
2 teaspoons butter
2 whole wheat English muffins, split and toasted
2 slices Cheddar cheese

1. Cook sausage according to package directions; set aside and keep warm.

2. Beat eggs, salt and pepper in small bowl. Melt butter in small skillet over low heat. Pour eggs into skillet; cook and stir gently until just set.

3. Place cheese on bottom halves of English muffins; top with sausage and scrambled eggs. Serve immediately.   *Makes 2 sandwiches*

Tip: Turkey sausage breakfast patties may vary in size. If patties are small, use two patties for each sandwich.

maple apple oatmeal

 2 cups apple juice
1½ cups water
 ⅓ cup AUNT JEMIMA® Syrup
 ½ teaspoon ground cinnamon
 ¼ teaspoon salt (optional)
 2 cups QUAKER® Oats (quick or old fashioned, uncooked)
 1 cup chopped fresh unpeeled apple (about 1 medium)

In a 3-quart saucepan, bring juice, water, syrup, cinnamon and, if desired, salt to a boil. Stir in oats and apple. Return to a boil; reduce heat to medium-low. Cook about 1 minute for quick oats (or 5 minutes for old fashioned oats) or until most of liquid is absorbed, stirring occasionally. Let stand until of desired consistency.   *Makes 4 servings*

quick breakfast sandwich

munchin'
lunches

sandwich monsters

1 package (about 16 ounces) refrigerated biscuits (8 count)
1 cup shredded mozzarella cheese
⅓ cup sliced mushrooms
2 ounces pepperoni slices, quartered (about 35 slices)
½ cup pizza sauce
1 egg, beaten

1. Preheat oven to 350°F. Line baking sheet with parchment paper or foil.

2. Separate dough into individual biscuits; set one biscuit aside. Roll out each remaining biscuit into 7-inch circle on lightly floured surface. Top half of each circle evenly with cheese, mushrooms, pepperoni and sauce, leaving ½-inch border. Fold dough over filling to form half moon shape; crimp edges closed with fork. Brush tops with egg.

3. Split remaining biscuit horizontally and cut each half into eight ¼-inch strips. For each sandwich, roll two strips dough into spirals to create eyes. Divide remaining two strips dough into seven pieces to create noses. Arrange eyes along straight edge of each sandwich; place nose between eyes. Brush eyes and nose with egg. Place on prepared baking sheet.

4. Bake 20 to 25 minutes or until golden brown. Let stand 3 to 5 minutes before serving. Serve warm with additional pizza sauce.

Makes 7 sandwiches

Tip: Don't worry about leaking sauce or cheese—it will look like it's coming from the monster's mouth!

sandwich monsters

chicken corndog bites

1 package (about 11 ounces) refrigerated corn breadstick dough (8 count)
1 package (10 ounces) Italian-seasoned cooked chicken breast strips
Mustard
Ketchup

1. Preheat oven to 375°F. Line baking sheet with parchment paper or foil.

2. Unroll dough and separate into individual breadsticks. Roll out each breadstick into 7×1½-inch rectangle (¼ inch thick). Cut each piece of dough in half crosswise to form 16 pieces total.

3. Cut chicken strips in half crosswise. Place one piece chicken on each piece of dough; wrap dough around chicken and seal, pressing edges together tightly. Place seam side down on prepared baking sheet.

4. Bake 15 to 17 minutes or until light golden brown. Decorate with mustard and ketchup. Serve warm with additional mustard and ketchup for dipping.

Makes 16 bites

ham, apple and cheese turnovers

1¼ cups chopped cooked ham
¾ cup finely chopped apple
¾ cup (3 ounces) shredded reduced-fat Cheddar cheese
1 tablespoon brown mustard (optional)
1 package (about 14 ounces) refrigerated pizza dough

1. Preheat oven to 400°F. Spray large baking sheet with nonstick cooking spray. Combine ham, apple, cheese and mustard in medium bowl.

2. Roll out pizza dough into 15×10-inch rectangle on lightly floured surface. Cut into six (5-inch) squares. Top squares evenly with ham mixture. Moisten edges with water. Fold dough over filling; press edges to seal. Place on prepared baking sheet.

3. Prick tops of each turnover with fork. Bake about 15 minutes or until golden brown. Serve warm or cool 1 hour on wire rack.   *Makes 6 servings*

Prep Time: 15 minutes
Bake Time: 15 minutes

chicken corndog bites

spotted butterfly sandwich

2 slices raisin bread
2 tablespoons cream cheese, softened
1 teaspoon honey
⅛ teaspoon cinnamon
1 baby carrot
½ stalk celery
2 carrot strips
2 dried apricots

1. Stack bread slices and cut diagonally into triangles. Place on plate with points facing in to form butterfly wings.

2. Combine cream cheese, honey and cinnamon in small bowl. Roll cream cheese mixture into 2 balls and place between bread slices at inside points, pressing down at points to lift top slice of bread.

3. Place baby carrot in center of bread slices to create body. Cut strips from celery for antennae. Decorate wings with carrot strips and apricots.

Makes 1 sandwich

ham & cheese quesadillas

½ cup (2 ounces) shredded Monterey Jack cheese
½ cup (2 ounces) shredded Cheddar cheese
4 (10-inch) flour tortillas
4 ounces finely chopped cooked ham
¼ cup chopped canned green chiles
Salsa (optional)

1. Combine cheeses; sprinkle evenly over 2 tortillas. Top with ham, chiles and remaining 2 tortillas.

2. Heat large skillet over medium heat. Add 1 quesadilla; cook about 2 minutes or until cheese melts and bottom is browned. Turn; cook until browned. Remove and keep warm while cooking remaining quesadilla. Cut each quesadilla into 8 wedges. Serve with salsa. *Makes 2 servings*

spotted butterfly sandwich

a-b-c minestrone

1 tablespoon olive oil
1 medium onion, chopped
2 medium carrots, chopped
1 small zucchini, chopped
½ teaspoon dried Italian seasoning
4 cups chicken broth
1 jar (1 pound 10 ounces) RAGÚ® OLD WORLD STYLE® Pasta Sauce
1 can (15½ ounces) cannellini or white kidney beans, rinsed and drained
1 cup alphabet pasta

1. In 4-quart saucepan, heat olive oil over medium heat and cook onion, carrots and zucchini, stirring frequently, 5 minutes or until vegetables are tender. Add Italian seasoning and cook, stirring occasionally, 1 minute. Add broth and Pasta Sauce and bring to a boil. Stir in beans and pasta. Cook, stirring occasionally, 10 minutes or until pasta is tender.

2. Serve, if desired, with chopped parsley and grated Parmesan cheese.

Makes 8 servings

sammich swirls

1 package (11 ounces) refrigerated French bread dough
Salt-free seasoning mix (optional)
Yellow mustard
4 slices light bologna
4 slices reduced-fat provolone cheese
2 teaspoons grated Parmesan cheese

1. Preheat oven to 350°F. Roll out dough into 12×10-inch rectangle. Sprinkle with seasoning, if desired. Dot with mustard.

2. Top dough alternately with bologna and provolone, overlapping edges. Starting from long side, roll up dough jelly-roll style; pinch seam to seal. Place roll, seam side down, on baking sheet. Sprinkle with Parmesan.

3. Bake 25 to 30 minutes or until puffy and browned. Let cool before slicing.

Makes 10 slices

a-b-c minestrone

corny face

 1 corn tortilla
 1 slice provolone cheese *or* 3 tablespoons shredded Cheddar cheese
 ½ large dill pickle, cut at an angle
 2 slices cucumber
 2 pitted black olives
 2 tablespoons shredded carrot

1. Spray nonstick skillet with nonstick cooking spray; heat over medium heat. Place tortilla in skillet; top with cheese. Heat 1 minute; fold tortilla in half, enclosing cheese.

2. Cook tortilla 1 minute per side or until cheese is melted and tortilla is lightly browned. Place tortilla on plate, rounded side down. Place pickle partially over tortilla at center for nose. Arrange cucumber slices, olives and carrot to resemble eyes and eyebrows.   *Makes 1 serving*

bowled over salad

 2 cups elbow macaroni
 1 cup fresh or frozen peas
 ½ cup chopped tomato
 ½ cup Italian dressing
 ½ cup (2 ounces) shredded Cheddar cheese
 ⅓ cup bacon, cooked and crumbled (optional)
 ¼ cup chopped green onion
 3 cups chopped lettuce

1. Cook pasta according to package directions; drain and rinse with cold water.

2. Combine pasta, peas, tomato, dressing, cheese, bacon, if desired, and green onion in large serving bowl. Place lettuce over pasta; cover with plastic wrap. Chill 4 to 6 hours.

3. Toss gently just before serving.   *Makes 6 servings*

Serving Suggestion: For an easy, portable lunchtime salad, assemble in individual resealable bowls.

corny face

turkey bacon mini wafflewiches

1 teaspoon Dijon mustard
1 teaspoon honey
8 frozen mini waffles (2 pieces, divided into individual waffles)
2 thin slices deli turkey, cut into thin strips
2 tablespoons cooked and crumbled bacon or bacon bits
4 teaspoons shredded Cheddar or mozzarella cheese
2 teaspoons butter

1. Combine mustard and honey in small bowl. Spread small amount of mustard mixture on one side of 4 waffles. Top each waffle with turkey; sprinkle with bacon and cheese. Top with remaining 4 waffles.

2. Melt butter in medium nonstick skillet over medium heat. Cook sandwiches 3 to 4 minutes per side, pressing with back of spatula, until cheese melts and waffles are golden. *Makes 2 servings*

cold pizza rolls

2 tablespoons cornmeal, divided
1 package (about 14 ounces) refrigerated pizza dough
6 ounces thinly sliced Canadian bacon
⅓ cup crushed pineapple, drained
⅓ cup pizza sauce
3 pieces (1 ounce each) string cheese

1. Preheat oven to 400°F. Spray large baking sheet with nonstick cooking spray. Lightly sprinkle with 1 tablespoon cornmeal.

2. Roll out pizza dough into 16½×11-inch rectangle on lightly floured surface. Lightly sprinkle with remaining 1 tablespoon cornmeal. Cut into six squares. Top each square with bacon, pineapple and pizza sauce.

3. Cut each piece of string cheese in half. Place one piece of cheese in center of each square. Bring up two opposite sides of each square and seal. Place rolls, seam side down, on prepared baking sheet. Crimp ends of rolls to seal.

4. Bake 15 to 17 minutes or until browned. Cool on wire rack. Wrap rolls in plastic wrap; refrigerate 2 hours or overnight. *Makes 6 pizza rolls*

turkey bacon mini wafflewiches

inside-out breadsticks

1 package (about 11 ounces) refrigerated breadsticks (12 count)
1 package (8 ounces) reduced-fat cream cheese, softened
1 to 2 tablespoons milk
¼ cup finely chopped carrot
2 tablespoons minced chives or green onions
12 slices deli ham, roast beef, turkey or chicken

1. Bake breadsticks according to package directions; cool.

2. Beat cream cheese with enough milk to make mixture spreadable. Stir in carrot and chives. Spread rounded tablespoon cream cheese mixture over each ham slice. Roll ham slices around breadsticks. Wrap tightly in plastic wrap; refrigerate until ready to serve.   *Makes 6 servings*

Note: Cream cheese spread can be made ahead and refrigerated for up to two days.

Variation: Use the cream cheese spread as a dip for broccoli spears or celery sticks. For dipping consistency, thin the cream cheese with additional 1 to 2 tablespoons milk.

quick tip

*These breadsticks can be part of a tasty school lunch,
but always keep food safety in mind when you're packing
lunches for your kids. Include a frozen juice box or frozen gel
pack in the lunchbox to keep the breadsticks cool.*

inside-out breadsticks

pizza dippin' strips

1 package (13.8 ounces) refrigerated pizza crust dough
15 thin slices pepperoni
1 cup shredded mozzarella cheese (about 4 ounces)
1 jar (1 pound 10 ounces) RAGÚ® Organic Pasta Sauce, heated

1. Preheat oven to 400°F.

2. On greased baking sheet, roll pizza dough into 12×9-inch rectangle. Fold edges over to make ¾-inch crust. Bake 7 minutes.

3. Evenly top pizza crust with pepperoni, then cheese. Bake an additional 8 minutes or until cheese is melted. Let stand 2 minutes.

4. Cut pizza in half lengthwise, then into 1½-inch strips. Serve with Pasta Sauce, heated, for dipping.   *Makes 16 strips*

Prep Time: 10 minutes
Cook Time: 15 minutes

kids' quesadillas

8 slices American cheese
8 (10-inch) flour tortillas
½ pound thinly sliced deli turkey
6 tablespoons *French's*® Honey Mustard
2 tablespoons melted butter
¼ teaspoon paprika

1. To prepare 1 quesadilla, arrange 2 slices of cheese on 1 tortilla. Top with ¼ of turkey. Spread with *1½ tablespoons* mustard, then top with another tortilla. Prepare 3 more quesadillas with remaining ingredients.

2. Combine butter and paprika. Brush one side of tortilla with butter mixture. Preheat 12-inch nonstick skillet over medium-high heat. Place tortilla butter side down and cook 2 minutes. Brush top of tortilla with butter mixture and turn over. Cook 1½ minutes or until golden brown. Repeat with remaining 3 quesadillas.

3. Slice into wedges before serving.   *Makes 4 servings*

pizza dippin' strips

super peanut butter sandwiches

⅔ cup peanut butter
2 tablespoons toasted wheat germ
1 tablespoon honey
8 slices firm-texture whole wheat or multi-grain bread
1 ripe banana, sliced
½ cup egg substitute *or* 2 eggs, beaten
⅓ cup orange juice
1 tablespoon grated orange peel
1 tablespoon butter

1. Combine peanut butter, wheat germ and honey in small bowl. Spread evenly on one side of each bread slice.

2. Place banana slices over peanut butter mixture on 4 bread slices. Top with remaining bread slices, peanut butter side down. Lightly press together.

3. Combine egg substitute, orange juice and orange peel in shallow dish. Dip sandwiches in egg mixture, coating both sides.

4. Melt butter in large nonstick skillet over medium heat. Cook sandwiches until golden brown, turning once. Serve immediately.   *Makes 4 servings*

bacon & tomato melts

4 slices cooked bacon
4 slices (1 ounce each) Cheddar cheese
1 tomato, sliced
4 slices whole wheat bread
2 teaspoons butter, melted

1. Layer 2 slices bacon, 2 slices cheese and tomato slices on 2 bread slices; top with remaining bread slices. Brush sandwiches with butter.

2. Heat large grill pan or skillet over medium heat. Add sandwiches; press lightly with spatula or weigh down with small plate. Cook 4 to 5 minutes per side or until cheese melts and sandwiches are golden brown.

Makes 2 sandwiches

super peanut butter sandwich

stuffed corn bread

1¼ cups all-purpose flour
¾ cup yellow cornmeal
2 tablespoons sugar
2 teaspoons baking powder
½ teaspoon salt
1 cup milk
¼ cup vegetable oil
1 egg
½ cup (2 ounces) diced Cheddar cheese, divided
2 thin slices deli ham, diced
¼ cup tomato or pasta sauce

1. Preheat oven to 350°F. Spray 3 mini (5×3-inch) loaf pans with nonstick cooking spray.

2. Combine flour, cornmeal, sugar, baking powder and salt in medium bowl. Whisk milk, oil and egg in small bowl until well blended. Pour milk mixture over flour mixture; stir just until moistened.

3. Spoon half of batter evenly into prepared pans. Layer with half of cheese, ham and tomato sauce; top with remaining batter and cheese.

4. Bake about 30 minutes or until edges are browned and toothpick inserted near centers comes out clean. Cool in pans on wire racks 5 minutes. Remove from pans; slice and serve warm. *Makes 6 servings*

Prep Time: 20 minutes
Bake Time: 30 minutes

stuffed corn bread

waffled grilled cheese

2 tablespoons butter
2 slices bread
1 teaspoon mustard
1 slice cheese
1 slice ham

1. Preheat waffle iron. Spread 1 tablespoon butter on one side of each bread slice. Spread mustard on other side of each bread slice. Layer cheese and ham over mustard. Top with remaining bread slice, mustard side down.

2. Spray waffle iron with nonstick cooking spray. Place sandwich in waffle iron; close lid. Cook 3 to 5 minutes or until top is browned and cheese is melted.

Makes 1 serving

apple-cheddar panini

1 tablespoon butter
2 cups thinly sliced apples*
¼ teaspoon ground cinnamon
8 teaspoons apple jelly
8 slices egg bread
4 slices (1 ounce each) mild Cheddar cheese

Use sweet apples such as Fuji or Royal Gala.

1. Melt butter in large nonstick skillet over medium heat. Add apples; sprinkle with cinnamon. Cook and stir 5 minutes or until apples are tender and golden. Remove from skillet; wipe skillet with paper towel.

2. Spread 2 teaspoons apple jelly on each of 4 bread slices; top with 1 slice cheese. Top with apples and remaining bread slices.

3. Heat same skillet over medium heat. Add sandwiches; press lightly with spatula or weigh down with small plate. Cook sandwiches 4 to 5 minutes per side or until cheese is melted and sandwiches are golden brown.

Makes 4 sandwiches

waffled grilled cheese

veggie wedgies

2 tablespoons olive oil
1 small onion, thinly sliced
1 small red bell pepper, thinly sliced
1 jar (1 pound 10 ounces) RAGÚ® Organic Pasta Sauce
4 (10-inch) burrito-size flour tortillas
1 cup shredded mozzarella cheese (about 4 ounces)

1. In 12-inch nonstick skillet, heat 1 tablespoon olive oil over medium-high heat and cook onion and red pepper, stirring occasionally, 4 minutes or until softened. Reduce heat to medium, then stir in 1½ cups Pasta Sauce. Simmer, stirring occasionally, 5 minutes or until sauce is thickened. Evenly spread sauce mixture on tortillas, leaving 1-inch border. Then top with cheese and fold in half; set aside. Clean skillet.

2. In same skillet, heat remaining 1 tablespoon olive oil over medium heat and cook quesadillas, 2 at a time, turning once, 4 minutes or until golden brown and cheese is melted. Cut quesadillas into wedges and serve with remaining Pasta Sauce, heated.   *Makes 4 servings*

Tip: Quesadillas can also be baked. Place folded filled tortillas on baking sheet and bake in preheated 425°F oven 5 minutes or until cheese is melted.

roarin' roast beef inside-out sandwiches

4 large leaves lettuce or Boston lettuce
4 thin slices deli roast beef
4 thin slices Cheddar or Muenster cheese
2 tablespoons barbecue sauce or mayonnaise
⅓ cup shredded carrot
4 (5- to 7-inch) plain crisp breadsticks

1. Top each lettuce leaf with 1 slice roast beef and 1 slice cheese. Spread with barbecue sauce and sprinkle with carrot.

2. Place one breadstick on one end of each stack; roll up. Serve immediately.
Makes 4 sandwiches

veggie wedgies

fruit slaw

  1 package (16 ounces) coleslaw mix
  1 Granny Smith apple, cut into matchstick strips
  1 D'Anjou pear, cut into matchstick strips
  1 cup sliced strawberries
  ⅓ cup lemon juice
  2 tablespoons light mayonnaise
  1 tablespoon sugar
  2 teaspoons poppy seeds
  1 teaspoon Dijon mustard
  ¼ teaspoon salt

1. Combine coleslaw mix, apple, pear and strawberries in large bowl.

2. Whisk lemon juice, mayonnaise, sugar, poppy seeds, mustard and salt in small bowl. Pour dressing over cabbage mixture and toss gently. Serve immediately. *Makes 7 cups*

feelin' good vegetable soup

  8 ounces ground turkey or ground beef
  1 can (about 14 ounces) reduced-sodium chicken or beef broth
  1 can (8 ounces) tomato sauce
  ½ cup uncooked small shell pasta
  1 teaspoon chili powder or Cajun seasoning
  ½ teaspoon dried basil
  ⅛ teaspoon garlic powder
  1½ cups frozen mixed vegetables

1. Brown turkey in medium saucepan over medium-high heat 6 to 8 minutes, stirring to break up meat; drain fat. Stir in broth, tomato sauce, pasta, chili powder, basil and garlic powder. Bring to a boil. Reduce heat; simmer, covered, 5 minutes.

2. Stir in frozen vegetables; bring to a boil. Simmer, covered, 5 minutes or until pasta is tender. Serve immediately. *Makes 4 servings*

fruit slaw

giggle jiggle parfaits

  3 envelopes unflavored gelatin
1½ cups water
  ¾ cup frozen pineapple-orange-apple juice concentrate or passion fruit juice concentrate (about half of 11½-ounce can)
     Food coloring (optional)
  3 cups mixed fresh berries (blueberries, blackberries and/or raspberries)
  2 containers (6 ounces each) orange cream or lemon low-fat yogurt

1. Spray 8-inch square baking dish with nonstick cooking spray. Sprinkle gelatin over water in small saucepan; let stand 5 minutes.

2. Cook and stir gelatin mixture over medium heat until boiling. Remove from heat; stir in juice concentrate and food coloring, if desired, until concentrate melts. Pour into prepared baking dish. Cover and refrigerate about 4 hours or until firm.

3. Use 1- to 1½-inch cookie cutters to cut gelatin mixture into shapes. Remove shapes from baking dish.

4. Layer gelatin shapes, berries and yogurt in six parfait glasses. Serve immediately. *Makes 6 servings*

Prep Time: 15 minutes
Chill Time: 4 hours

giggle jiggle parfaits

banana caterpillars

2 medium bananas
¼ cup peanut butter
¼ cup flaked coconut
4 raisins
Thin pretzel sticks

1. Cut each banana crosswise into 10 slices. Assemble caterpillar by spreading slices with peanut butter and pressing together.

2. Sprinkle half of coconut over each caterpillar and press lightly to coat bananas. Use additional peanut butter to attach raisins on one end for eyes. Break pretzel sticks into small pieces; press between banana slices to create legs and antennae. *Makes 2 servings*

Tip: Kids can also be creative and add other types of sliced fruits (strawberries, apples, pears) to their caterpillars.

snickerdoodle snack mix

1 bag popped JOLLY TIME Healthy Pop 94% Fat Free Butter Flavor Microwave Pop Corn, popped (about 12 cups)
1½ tablespoons cinnamon-sugar
2 cups graham cracker sticks
½ cup cinnamon chips or semi-sweet chocolate chips

1. Pop popcorn according to package directions. Open bag carefully and pour into bowl; discard unpopped kernels. Sprinkle popcorn with cinnamon-sugar; toss until evenly coated.

2. Add graham cracker sticks to bowl with popcorn; allow mixture to cool for 5 minutes.

3. Toss in cinnamon chips or semi-sweet chocolate chips. Store in covered container. *Makes about 12 cups*

banana caterpillar

ham & cheese snacks

8 thin slices ham (about 6 ounces total)
2 tablespoons honey mustard
8 thin slices Muenster cheese (about 4 ounces total)
   Thin pretzel crisps or favorite crackers

1. Spread each ham slice with about ¾ teaspoon mustard. Top 1 slice ham with 1 slice cheese; top with second slice of ham and cheese.

2. Starting with long side, roll up each ham and cheese stack jelly-roll style. Wrap tightly in plastic wrap; refrigerate 30 minutes or up to 24 hours.

3. Cut each ham and cheese roll into ½-inch slices. Serve on pretzel crisps.
Makes 4 servings

cinnamon toast poppers

6 cups fresh bread cubes* (1-inch cubes)
2 tablespoons butter, melted
1 tablespoon plus 1½ teaspoons sugar
½ teaspoon ground cinnamon

Use a firm sourdough, whole wheat or semolina bread.

1. Preheat oven to 325°F. Place bread cubes in large bowl. Drizzle with butter; toss to coat.

2. Combine sugar and cinnamon in small bowl. Sprinkle over bread cubes; mix well.

3. Spread bread cubes in single layer on ungreased baking sheet. Bake 25 minutes or until bread is golden and fragrant, stirring once or twice. Serve warm or at room temperature.
Makes 12 servings

ham & cheese snacks

cherry chocolate frosty

1 container (6 ounces) chocolate yogurt
½ cup frozen dark sweet cherries
⅛ to ¼ teaspoon almond extract

1. Combine yogurt, cherries and almond extract in blender; blend about 30 seconds or until smooth.

2. Pour into glass; serve immediately.

Makes 1 serving

taco boulders

2¼ cups biscuit baking mix
1 cup (4 ounces) shredded taco cheese
2 tablespoons canned diced green chiles, drained
⅔ cup milk
3 tablespoons butter, melted
¼ teaspoon chili powder
¼ teaspoon garlic powder

1. Preheat oven to 425°F. Line baking sheet with parchment paper or spray with nonstick cooking spray.

2. Combine baking mix, cheese and chiles in large bowl. Stir in milk just until moistened. Drop dough by rounded tablespoons into 12 mounds on prepared baking sheet.

3. Bake 11 to 13 minutes or until golden brown. Meanwhile, combine melted butter, chili powder and garlic powder in small bowl. Remove biscuits to wire rack; immediately brush with butter mixture. Serve warm.

Makes 12 biscuits

Prep Time: 5 minutes
Bake Time: 11 minutes

cherry chocolate frosty

happy apple salsa with cinnamon pita chips

2 teaspoons sugar
¼ teaspoon cinnamon
2 pita bread rounds, split
1 tablespoon jelly or jam
1 medium apple, diced
1 tablespoon finely diced celery
1 tablespoon finely diced carrot
1 tablespoon raisins
1 teaspoon lemon juice

1. Preheat oven to 350°F. Combine sugar and cinnamon in small bowl.

2. Cut pitas into wedges; place on ungreased baking sheet. Spray with nonstick cooking spray; sprinkle with cinnamon-sugar. Bake 10 minutes or until lightly browned; set aside to cool.

3. Meanwhile, place jelly in medium microwavable bowl; microwave on HIGH 10 seconds. Stir in apple, celery, carrot, raisins and lemon juice. Serve salsa with pita chips. *Makes 3 servings*

gelatin fruit smoothies

2 cups reduced-fat (2%) milk
2 cups fresh strawberries, hulled
1 package (4-serving size) strawberry gelatin

Combine milk, strawberries and gelatin in blender; blend 1 to 2 minutes or until smooth and frothy. *Makes 4 servings*

Tips: Try your favorite gelatin and fruit combination. Fruits such as peaches, raspberries and oranges work well. This is also a great way to use up overripe fruit.

happy apple salsa with cinnamon pita chips

super salami twists

1 egg
1 tablespoon milk
1 cup finely chopped hard salami (about 4 ounces)
2 tablespoons yellow cornmeal
1 teaspoon Italian seasoning
1 package (about 11 ounces) refrigerated breadstick dough
¾ cup marinara sauce, heated

1. Preheat oven to 375°F. Line baking sheet with foil or parchment paper.

2. Beat egg and milk in shallow dish until well blended. Combine salami, cornmeal and Italian seasoning in separate shallow dish.

3. Unroll breadstick dough. Separate into 12 pieces along perforations. Roll each piece of dough in egg mixture, then in salami mixture, gently pressing salami into dough. Twist each piece of dough twice and place on prepared baking sheet.

4. Bake 13 to 15 minutes or until golden brown. Remove to wire rack; cool 5 minutes. Serve warm with marinara sauce for dipping.   *Makes 12 twists*

Prep Time: 10 minutes
Bake Time: 13 minutes

peanut butter-apple wraps

¾ cup creamy peanut butter
4 (7-inch) whole wheat or spinach tortillas
¾ cup finely chopped apple
⅓ cup shredded carrot
⅓ cup low-fat granola without raisins
1 tablespoon toasted wheat germ

Spread peanut butter on one side of each tortilla. Sprinkle evenly with apple, carrot, granola and wheat germ. Roll up tightly; cut in half. Serve immediately or wrap in plastic wrap and refrigerate until ready to serve.

Makes 4 servings

super salami twists

nutty fruit salad

1 large apple, cut into 24 pieces
1 tablespoon lemon juice
1 can (8 ounces) pineapple chunks in juice
24 miniature marshmallows
1 cup seedless grapes
½ cup plain yogurt
½ cup creamy peanut butter

1. Combine apple and lemon juice in small bowl; toss to coat. Drain pineapple, reserving 4 teaspoons juice.

2. Thread apple pieces, marshmallows, grapes and pineapple on small skewers.

3. Whisk yogurt and peanut butter in separate small bowl until smooth. Stir in reserved pineapple juice. Serve fruit skewers with peanut butter sauce for dipping.   *Makes 6 servings*

Tips: Six-inch wooden skewers can be used for this recipe. Or omit skewers; spoon fruit and marshmallows into 6 small serving dishes and drizzle with peanut butter sauce.

Prep Time: 15 minutes

mud hole dunk

4 cups fresh strawberries, cut-up fresh pineapple and seedless grapes
1 cup prepared creamy chocolate frosting*
Assorted decorator sprinkles or flaked coconut

Do not use whipped frosting.

1. Line baking sheet with waxed paper. Pat fruit dry with paper towels.

2. Place frosting in small microwavable bowl; microwave on HIGH 15 to 20 seconds or until melted, stirring once.

3. Dip fruit halfway into frosting, allowing excess to drip off. Roll in sprinkles or coconut; place on prepared baking sheet. Refrigerate about 10 minutes or until frosting is set.   *Makes 8 servings*

nutty fruit salad

chocolate panini bites

¼ cup chocolate hazelnut spread
4 slices hearty sandwich bread or Italian bread

1. Preheat indoor grill.* Spread chocolate hazelnut spread evenly over 2 slices bread; top with remaining slices.

2. Spray sandwiches with nonstick cooking spray. Grill 2 to 3 minutes or until bread is golden brown. Cut sandwiches into triangles. *Makes 4 servings*

*Panini can also be made on the stove in a ridged grill pan or nonstick skillet. Cook sandwiches over medium heat about 2 minutes per side.

Chocolate Raspberry Panini Bites: Spread 2 slices bread with raspberry jam or preserves; spread remaining slices with chocolate hazelnut spread. Cook sandwiches as directed above; watch grill or pan closely because jam burns easily.

pita cheese straws

3 (6-inch) pita bread rounds
2 tablespoons butter, melted
1 clove garlic, minced
1 teaspoon Italian seasoning
¼ cup grated Parmesan cheese
French onion dip
Celery sticks and baby carrots

1. Preheat oven to 350°F. Split pitas in half horizontally. Combine butter, garlic and Italian seasoning in small bowl.

2. Brush tops of pitas with butter mixture; sprinkle with Parmesan cheese. Cut into ½-inch strips with pizza cutter. Arrange strips in single layer on ungreased baking sheet.

3. Bake 8 to 10 minutes or until edges are deep golden brown. Serve with dip and vegetables. *Makes 6 servings*

chocolate panini bites

edamame hummus

1 package (16 ounces) frozen shelled edamame, thawed
2 green onions, roughly chopped (about ½ cup)
½ cup loosely packed fresh cilantro
3 to 4 tablespoons water
2 tablespoons canola oil
1½ tablespoons fresh lime juice
1 tablespoon honey
2 cloves garlic
1 teaspoon salt
¼ teaspoon black pepper
Rice crackers, baby carrots, cucumber slices and sugar snap peas

1. Combine edamame, green onions, cilantro, 3 tablespoons water, oil, lime juice, honey, garlic, salt and pepper in food processor; process until smooth. Add additional water if necessary to thin out and smooth dip.

2. Serve with crackers and vegetables for dipping. Store leftover dip in refrigerator up to 4 days.   *Makes about 2 cups*

watermelon kebobs

18 (1-inch) cubes seedless watermelon
6 ounces (1-inch cubes) fat-free turkey breast
6 ounces (1-inch cubes) reduced-fat Cheddar cheese
6 (6-inch) bamboo skewers

Thread cubes of watermelon onto skewers, alternating between cubes of turkey and cheese.   *Makes 6 servings*

Favorite recipe from **National Watermelon Promotion Board**

edamame hummus

mini cheese burritos

½ cup canned refried beans
4 (8-inch) flour tortillas
½ cup chunky salsa
4 (¾-ounce) reduced-fat Cheddar cheese sticks*

Reduced-fat Cheddar cheese block can be substituted; cut cheese into 2×¼×¼-inch sticks.

1. Spread beans over half of each tortilla, leaving ½-inch border around edges. Spoon salsa over beans.

2. Place cheese stick on one side of each tortilla. Fold one edge of each tortilla over cheese stick; roll up. Place burritos, seam side down, on microwavable plate.

3. Microwave on HIGH 1 to 2 minutes or until cheese is melted. Let stand 1 to 2 minutes before serving.   *Makes 4 servings*

whole-grain cereal bars

5 to 6 cups assorted whole-grain cereals
1 package (10 ounces) large marshmallows
¼ cup (½ stick) butter
¼ cup uncooked old-fashioned oats

1. Crush large chunks of cereal by placing in large resealable food storage bag and lightly rolling over bag with rolling pin. Generously grease 13×9-inch baking pan.

2. Melt marshmallows and butter in large saucepan over medium-low heat, stirring occasionally. Remove saucepan from heat.

3. Stir in cereal until well blended. Using buttered hands or waxed paper to prevent sticking, pat cereal mixture evenly into prepared pan. Sprinkle with oats. Cool at room temperature until firm. Cut into bars.

Makes about 24 bars

mini cheese burritos

watermelon banana split

- 2 bananas
- 1 medium watermelon
- 1 cup fresh blueberries
- 1 cup diced fresh pineapple
- 1 cup sliced fresh strawberries
- ¼ cup caramel fruit dip
- ¼ cup honey roasted almonds

Peel bananas and cut in half lengthwise, then cut each piece in half. For each serving, lay 2 banana pieces against sides of shallow dish. Using ice cream scooper, place three watermelon "scoops" in between banana pieces in each dish. Remove seeds, if necessary. Top each watermelon "scoop" with different fresh fruit topping. Drizzle caramel fruit dip over all. Sprinkle with almonds.
Makes 4 servings

Favorite recipe from **National Watermelon Promotion Board**

frozen apple slushies

- ½ cup frozen unsweetened apple juice concentrate
- 1 large Red Delicious apple, peeled and cut into chunks
- 1 cup 100% cranberry juice, chilled
- ⅛ teaspoon ground cinnamon
- 3 cups ice cubes

Combine apple juice concentrate, apple, cranberry juice and cinnamon in blender; blend until smooth. Add ice cubes, 1 cup at a time, blending after each addition until smooth. Serve with straws or spoons.
Makes 4 servings

Tip: Freeze leftovers in 1-cup servings in small airtight microwavable containers. To serve, microwave each serving on HIGH 15 seconds; stir. Continue to microwave in 10-second increments until slushy.

watermelon banana split

peachy pops

1 package (16 ounces) frozen sliced peaches, softened (not thawed)
2 containers (6 ounces each) peach or vanilla yogurt
¼ cup honey
12 small paper cups
12 popsicle or lollipop sticks
   Colored sugar or sugar sprinkles

1. Combine peaches, yogurt and honey in food processor or blender; process about 20 seconds or until smooth.

2. Pour peach mixture into paper cups and place on baking sheet. Freeze 1 hour or until mixture begins to harden. Push popsicle stick into center of each cup; freeze an additional 3 hours or until firm.

3. Tear paper away from pops and roll in sugar or sprinkles. Serve immediately or return to freezer until ready to serve. *Makes 12 servings*

Prep Time: **20 minutes**
Freeze Time: **4 hours**

banana roll-ups

¼ cup creamy or crunchy almond butter
2 tablespoons mini chocolate chips
1 to 2 tablespoons milk
1 (8-inch) whole wheat flour tortilla
1 large banana, peeled

1. Combine almond butter, chocolate chips and 1 tablespoon milk in medium microwavable bowl. Microwave on MEDIUM (50%) 40 seconds; stir. Microwave 30 seconds more, if necessary, to melt chocolate. Add additional milk, if necessary, to reach desired spreading consistency.

2. Spread almond butter mixture over tortilla. Place banana on one side of tortilla and roll up tightly. Cut into 8 slices. *Makes 2 servings*

peachy pops

dynamite dinners

beanie burgers

  1 can (about 15 ounces) red kidney beans, rinsed and drained
  ½ cup chopped onion
  ⅓ cup uncooked quick oats
  1 tablespoon taco seasoning mix or mild chili powder
  1 egg
  ½ teaspoon salt
  4 slices cheese
  4 whole-grain hamburger buns, toasted
  4 leaves lettuce
  4 slices tomato
    Salsa, mayonnaise and mustard (optional)

1. Combine beans, onion, oats, taco seasoning mix, egg and salt in food processor. Process with on/off pulses until mixture is chunky, but before it becomes smooth. (Mixture may be made up to 1 day in advance. Cover and refrigerate until needed.)

2. Spray large skillet with nonstick cooking spray; heat over medium heat. Spoon bean mixture into four round patties in skillet, spreading mixture with back of spoon.

3. Cook burgers undisturbed 4 minutes; turn carefully with spatula. Place 1 slice cheese on each patty; cook 4 to 5 minutes. Place lettuce, burgers and tomato on buns; serve with salsa, mayonnaise and mustard.

Makes 4 servings

beanie burger

better-than-take-out fried rice

3 tablespoons reduced-sodium soy sauce
1 tablespoon rice vinegar
1/8 teaspoon red pepper flakes
1 medium red bell pepper, cored and seeded
1 cup green onions cut into 1-inch pieces
1 tablespoon grated fresh ginger
1½ teaspoons minced garlic
1 tablespoon peanut or vegetable oil
8 ounces boneless pork loin or tenderloin, cut into 1-inch pieces
2 cups packaged coleslaw mix
1 package (8½ ounces) cooked whole-grain brown rice

1. Combine soy sauce, vinegar and red pepper flakes in small bowl; mix well.

2. Cut bell pepper into decorative shapes using 1¼- to 1½-inch cookie cutters.

3. Stir-fry bell pepper, green onions, ginger and garlic in oil in large nonstick skillet or wok over medium-high heat 1 minute. Add pork; stir-fry 2 to 3 minutes or until pork is barely pink in center. Stir in coleslaw mix, rice and soy sauce mixture; cook and stir about 1 minute or until heated through.

Makes 4 servings

turkey tacos

1 cup chopped cooked turkey breast or chicken breast
½ cup chopped carrot
⅓ cup chopped celery
¼ cup (1 ounce) shredded taco cheese blend
3 tablespoons mayonnaise
2 tablespoons salsa
6 taco shells

Combine turkey, carrot, celery, cheese, mayonnaise and salsa in medium bowl. Spoon into taco shells.

Makes 6 servings

better-than-take-out fried rice

cheesy broccoli soup

    1 teaspoon olive oil
    ½ cup finely chopped onion
    1 cup water
 1½ teaspoons chicken bouillon granules
    3 cups small broccoli florets or thawed frozen chopped broccoli
    ½ cup evaporated skim milk
    ⅛ teaspoon ground red pepper
    2 ounces cubed light pasteurized process cheese product
    ¼ cup reduced-fat sour cream
    ⅛ teaspoon salt

1. Heat oil in medium saucepan over medium-high heat. Add onion; cook and stir 4 minutes or until translucent.

2. Add water and bouillon granules; bring to a boil over high heat. Add broccoli; return to a boil. Reduce heat; simmer, covered, 5 minutes or until broccoli is tender.

3. Whisk in milk and red pepper. Remove from heat; stir in cheese until melted. Stir in sour cream and salt.   *Makes 2 servings*

muffin pizza italiano

    1 sandwich-size English muffin, split, toasted
    2 tablespoons CONTADINA® Pizza Squeeze Pizza Sauce
    8 slices pepperoni
    ¼ cup sliced fresh mushrooms
    ¼ cup (1 ounce) shredded mozzarella cheese

1. Spread muffin halves with pizza sauce. Top with pepperoni, mushrooms and cheese.

2. Bake in preheated 400°F oven for 8 to 10 minutes or until cheese is melted.   *Makes 2 servings*

Prep Time: 5 minutes
Cook Time: 10 minutes

cheesy broccoli soup

polka dot lasagna skillet

1 pound ground turkey or beef
1 package lasagna and sauce meal kit
4 cups hot water
½ cup ricotta cheese
1 egg
3 tablespoons grated Parmesan cheese
2 tablespoons all-purpose flour
2 tablespoons chopped fresh parsley
½ teaspoon Italian seasoning
¼ teaspoon black pepper

1. Cook turkey in large skillet over medium high heat until no longer pink, stirring to break up meat; drain fat.

2. Stir in contents of meal kit and hot water; bring to a boil. Reduce heat to low; cover and cook 10 minutes.

3. Meanwhile, blend ricotta cheese, egg, Parmesan cheese, flour, parsley, Italian seasoning and pepper in small bowl until smooth. Drop tablespoonfuls of ricotta mixture over pasta; cover and cook 4 to 5 minutes or until dumplings are set. Remove from heat; let stand about 4 minutes before serving.

Makes 4 to 6 servings

golden chicken nuggets

1 pound boneless skinless chicken, cut into 1½-inch pieces
¼ cup *French's*® Honey Mustard
2 cups *French's*® French Fried Onions, finely crushed

1. Preheat oven to 400°F. Toss chicken with mustard in medium bowl.

2. Place French Fried Onions into resealable plastic food storage bag. Toss chicken in onions, a few pieces at a time, pressing gently to adhere.

3. Place nuggets in shallow baking pan. Bake 15 minutes or until chicken is no longer pink in center. Serve with additional honey mustard.

Makes 4 servings

polka dot lasagna skillet

sloppy joe burritos

1 pound ground beef
1 cup chopped bell pepper (red, green or a combination)
½ cup chopped onion
1 can (16 ounces) sloppy joe sauce
4 (7- or 8-inch) colored tortillas
1 tablespoon cider vinegar
1 teaspoon vegetable oil
1 teaspoon sugar
¼ teaspoon salt
2 cups coleslaw mix

1. Cook beef, bell pepper and onion in large skillet over medium heat until beef is no longer pink, stirring to break up meat. Drain fat. Stir in sauce; cook over low heat 3 minutes or until slightly thickened.

2. Whisk vinegar, oil, sugar and salt in medium bowl until well blended. Add coleslaw mix; toss to coat.

3. Divide beef mixture evenly among tortillas; top with coleslaw mixture. Roll up tortillas burrito-style, folding in sides to enclose filling.

Makes 4 servings

taco taters

1 pound ground beef
1 jar (1 pound 10 ounces) RAGÚ® Old World Style® Pasta Sauce
1 package (1¼ ounces) taco seasoning mix
6 large all-purpose potatoes, unpeeled and baked

1. In 12-inch skillet, brown ground beef over medium-high heat; drain. Stir in Pasta Sauce and taco seasoning mix and cook 5 minutes.

2. To serve, cut a lengthwise slice from top of each potato. Evenly spoon beef mixture onto each potato. Garnish, if desired, with shredded Cheddar cheese and sour cream.

Makes 6 servings

Prep Time: 5 minutes
Cook Time: 15 minutes

sloppy joe burrito

bbq chicken stromboli

1 rotisserie-roasted chicken* (2 to 2¼ pounds)
⅓ cup barbecue sauce
1 package (about 14 ounces) refrigerated pizza dough
1 cup (4 ounces) shredded Cheddar cheese
⅓ cup sliced green onions, divided

*If desired, use 8 ounces roast chicken breast from the deli, chopped, instead of the 2 cups shredded rotisserie chicken.

1. Remove and discard skin from chicken. Shred chicken using two forks; discard bones. (You should have about 4 cups shredded chicken.) Combine 2 cups chicken and barbecue sauce in medium bowl until well blended. Wrap and refrigerate or freeze remaining chicken for another use.

2. Preheat oven to 400°F. Lightly spray baking sheet with nonstick cooking spray. Unroll pizza dough on baking sheet; pat into 12×9-inch rectangle.

3. Spread chicken mixture lengthwise down center of dough, leaving 2½ inches on each side. Sprinkle with cheese and ¼ cup green onion. Fold long sides of dough over filling; press edges to seal.

4. Sprinkle with remaining green onion. Bake 19 to 22 minutes or until golden brown. Let stand 10 minutes before slicing.   *Makes 6 servings*

rings-on-your-fingers salad

1 package (about 9 ounces) refrigerated cheese tortellini
½ cup sliced carrot
½ red bell pepper, cut crosswise into rings
½ green bell pepper, cut crosswise into rings
½ cup cherry or grape tomatoes
4 tablespoons raspberry balsamic vinaigrette

1. Cook tortellini according to package directions. During last minute of cooking time, add carrot and bell peppers. Drain tortellini and vegetables; rinse under cold water. Drain thoroughly and place in serving bowls.

2. Top with tomatoes. Drizzle dressing over salad or serve on the side for dipping.   *Makes 4 servings*

bbq chicken stromboli

chili con corny

1 tablespoon vegetable oil
½ cup finely chopped onion
1 pound ground turkey
1 can (about 15 ounces) kidney beans, rinsed and drained
1 can (about 14 ounces) diced tomatoes
1 can (11 ounces) corn, drained
1 can (8 ounces) tomato sauce
2 teaspoons chili seasoning mix or taco seasoning
1 teaspoon ground cumin
1 teaspoon salt
¾ cup (3 ounces) shredded Cheddar cheese
2 cups corn chips

1. Heat oil in large skillet over medium heat. Add onion; cook and stir 2 minutes. Add turkey; cook until no longer pink, stirring to break up meat.

2. Stir in beans, tomatoes, corn, tomato sauce, chili seasoning mix, cumin and salt. Bring mixture to a simmer and cook 10 minutes, stirring frequently.

3. Divide chili among 4 serving bowls. Sprinkle cheese into center of bowls. Overlap corn chips around edges of bowls to create flower or sun.

Makes 4 servings

whipped sweet potatoes

2 large sweet potatoes (about 2 pounds)
2 tablespoons vanilla yogurt
2 tablespoons apple jelly
½ teaspoon salt

1. Pierce potatoes in several places with fork. Microwave on HIGH 10 minutes. Turn potatoes; microwave 5 minutes or until tender. Let stand 2 minutes; peel.

2. Place potatoes in medium bowl. Add yogurt, apple jelly and salt; mash with potato masher or fork until smooth. Whisk until light and fluffy.

Makes 4 servings

chili con corny

fish and "chips"

3 cups crisp rice cereal, divided
1 egg
1 tablespoon water
1 pound cod, haddock or other firm white fish fillets
1½ teaspoons Italian seasoning, divided
   Salt and black pepper
2 tablespoons butter, melted
2 medium zucchini, cut into sticks
1 package (8 ounces) carrot sticks
1 tablespoon olive oil

1. Preheat oven to 350°F. Spray large baking sheet with nonstick cooking spray or line with foil. Place 2 cups cereal in large resealable food storage bag and coarsely crush. Combine with remaining 1 cup cereal in large shallow dish. Beat egg and water in another large shallow dish.

2. Cut fish into pieces, 3 to 4 inches long and about 2 inches wide. Sprinkle with 1 teaspoon Italian seasoning, salt and pepper. Dip fish pieces into egg mixture; drain off excess and place in dish of cereal. Turn to coat all sides, pressing cereal onto fish. Place on prepared baking sheet; drizzle with butter.

3. Place zucchini and carrot sticks on same baking sheet in single layer. Drizzle with oil and sprinkle with remaining ½ teaspoon Italian seasoning, salt and pepper.

4. Bake 20 to 25 minutes or until fish is opaque in center and vegetables are tender.   *Makes 4 servings*

fish and "chips"

quick taco macaroni & cheese

1 pound lean ground beef or turkey
1 package (1 ounce) LAWRY'S® Taco Spices & Seasonings
1 package (1 pound) large elbow macaroni, cooked and drained
4 cups (16 ounces) shredded cheddar cheese
2 cups milk
3 eggs, beaten

In medium skillet, brown ground beef; drain fat. Stir in Taco Spices & Seasonings. Spray 13×9×2-inch baking dish with nonstick cooking spray. Layer half of macaroni in bottom of dish. Top with half of cheese. Spread taco meat over top and repeat layers of macaroni and cheese. In medium bowl, beat together milk and eggs. Pour egg mixture over top of casserole. Bake in preheated 350°F oven for 30 to 35 minutes or until golden brown.

Makes 6 to 8 servings

Variation: For spicier flavor, try using LAWRY'S® Chili Spices & Seasonings *or* LAWRY'S® Hot Taco Spices & Seasonings instead of Taco Spices & Seasonings.

chicken in a nest

8 ounces uncooked angel hair pasta
1 can (10 ounces) chicken breast in water, drained
1 package (6 ounces) whipped cream cheese with garden vegetables or garlic and herb spread
½ cup frozen peas
2 tablespoons milk
1 teaspoon salt
⅛ teaspoon pepper

1. Cook pasta according to package directions; drain and return to saucepan. Gently stir in chicken, cream cheese, peas, milk, salt and pepper.

2. Stir mixture over low heat until heated through. (If sauce is too thick, add milk until desired consistency is reached.) To serve, swirl pasta in center of serving dish with large fork. Spoon sauce and chicken into center of nest.

Makes 4 servings

quick taco macaroni & cheese

shrimp-tastic kabobs

1 small fresh pineapple
12 ounces large raw shrimp, peeled and deveined
1 medium red bell pepper, cut into 1½-inch pieces
½ teaspoon lemon pepper
3 tablespoons reduced-fat raspberry vinaigrette or Italian salad dressing

1. Spray cold grill grid with nonstick cooking spray. Preheat grill to medium heat. Remove and discard top from pineapple. Cut pineapple lengthwise into 8 wedges. Set 4 wedges aside. Peel and core remaining 4 wedges. Cut peeled wedges crosswise into ¾-inch slices.

2. Thread shrimp, peeled pineapple and bell pepper onto 16 (5- to 6-inch) wooden* or metal skewers, leaving small space between pieces. Sprinkle with lemon pepper.

3. Grill kabobs 5 to 8 minutes or until shrimp turn pink and opaque, brushing frequently with vinaigrette. Turn kabobs halfway through grilling time. To serve, stand 4 kabobs in each pineapple wedge.   *Makes 4 servings*

*If using wooden skewers, soak skewers in water for 20 minutes to prevent burning.

beanie weenies

1 can (about 15 ounces) light red kidney or pinto beans, rinsed and drained
1 cup frozen corn kernels
½ cup mild salsa
2 tablespoons water
2 teaspoons taco seasoning mix
4 turkey hot dogs, sliced
¼ cup shredded cheese
4 (6-inch) flour tortillas, warmed

1. Combine beans, corn, salsa, water and taco seasoning mix in large skillet; mix well. Bring to a simmer over medium heat.

2. Stir in sliced hot dogs; cook about 5 minutes or until heated through. Spoon into 4 serving bowls; top with cheese. Serve with warm tortillas.
                                                              Makes 4 servings

shrimp-tastic kabobs

crunch a bunch salad

2 tablespoons honey or sugar
1 tablespoon vegetable oil
1 tablespoon apple cider vinegar
½ teaspoon soy sauce or lemon juice
1 cup sugar snap peas, trimmed
1 carrot, peeled and thinly sliced
1 stalk celery, sliced
3 radishes, thinly sliced
4 cherry tomatoes, cut into quarters
4 teaspoons sliced almonds

1. Whisk honey, oil, vinegar and soy sauce in small bowl until well blended.

2. Arrange sugar snap peas, carrot, celery and radishes in 4 individual bowls. Top with tomatoes and almonds. Drizzle with dressing or serve on the side for dipping.

Makes 4 servings

calzone-on-a-stick

8 turkey or chicken sausage links (about 1½ pounds), cooked
8 wooden craft sticks
1 package (16.3 ounces) refrigerated grand-size biscuits
1 jar (1 pound 10 ounces) RAGÚ® OLD WORLD STYLE® Pasta Sauce
4 mozzarella cheese sticks, halved lengthwise

1. Preheat oven to 350°F. Insert craft stick halfway into each sausage; set aside.

2. Separate biscuits. On lightly floured surface, roll each biscuit into 7×4-inch oval. Place 2 tablespoons Pasta Sauce on long side of each oval. Top with sausage and ½ mozzarella stick. Fold dough over and pinch edges to seal. On greased baking sheet, arrange calzones seam-side down.

3. Bake 15 minutes or until golden. Serve with remaining Pasta Sauce, heated, for dipping.

Makes 8 servings

Prep Time: 20 minutes
Cook Time: 15 minutes

crunch a bunch salad

cheesy potato head

 4 small baking potatoes
⅓ cup sour cream
¼ teaspoon salt
⅛ teaspoon garlic powder
⅛ teaspoon black pepper
½ cup (2 ounces) shredded Cheddar cheese
¼ cup finely chopped broccoli
16 slices pimiento-stuffed olives
 4 small broccoli florets
 4 small pieces red bell pepper
 4 pretzel twists

1. Preheat oven to 425°F. Pierce potatoes several times with fork. Place in shallow baking pan; bake 55 to 65 minutes or until tender. Let stand 10 minutes.

2. Cut thin slice lengthwise from side of each potato; discard. Scoop pulp from potatoes into medium bowl, leaving ¼-inch shell.

3. Mash potato pulp with potato masher. Stir in sour cream, salt, garlic powder and black pepper; fold in cheese and broccoli. Spoon potato mixture into shells; return to pan. Bake, uncovered, 20 to 25 minutes or until heated through.

4. Create face on each potato using olive slices for eyes and ears, broccoli floret for nose and bell pepper for mouth.

5. Break bottom off of each pretzel twist. Press top of one pretzel into each potato to create glasses. *Makes 4 servings*

Prep Time: 20 minutes
Bake Time: 1 hour 15 minutes

cheesy potato head

bbq turkey minis

½ **cup panko bread crumbs**
½ **cup barbecue sauce, divided**
1 **egg, beaten**
1 **pound lean ground turkey**
1 **package (12 ounces) Hawaiian bread rolls, sliced horizontally**
   Lettuce
   Tomato slices
3 **slices American cheese, quartered**

1. Generously grease grill grid. Preheat grill to high heat.

2. Combine bread crumbs, ¼ cup barbecue sauce and egg in medium bowl; mix well. Add turkey; mix just until combined. Shape turkey mixture into 12 small ½-inch-thick burgers (¼ cup per burger).

3. Grill burgers, covered, 8 to 10 minutes, turning once during cooking. Brush with remaining ¼ cup barbecue sauce during last minute of cooking.

4. Top bottoms of buns with lettuce, tomato, burgers, cheese and tops of buns. *Makes 12 mini burgers*

Tip: Centers of burgers should reach 160°F before removing from grill; internal temperature will rise to 165°F upon standing.

silly face pizza

1 **(10-ounce) prebaked pizza crust**
1 **cup RAGÚ® OLD WORLD STYLE® Pasta Sauce**
1½ **cups shredded mozzarella cheese (about 6 ounces)**
   Silly Face Garnishes*

*For Silly Face Garnishes, use ½ cup cooked rotini pasta for hair, broccoli for eyebrows, roasted red peppers and peas for eyes, baby carrot half for nose and pepperoni slice for mouth.

1. Preheat oven to 450°F.

2. On baking sheet, arrange pizza crust. Evenly top with Pasta Sauce, then cheese and Silly Face Garnishes. Bake 12 minutes or until cheese is melted and crust is golden. *Makes 4 servings*

bbq turkey minis

not-so-sloppy joes

1 pound lean ground beef or turkey
⅓ cup finely chopped onion
⅓ cup shredded carrot
1 can (8 ounces) tomato sauce, divided
1 egg
½ teaspoon salt
½ teaspoon Italian seasoning
⅛ teaspoon black pepper
6 hot dog buns
6 slices mozzarella cheese, halved

1. Preheat oven to 350°F. Spray 13×9-inch baking pan with nonstick cooking spray.

2. Combine ground beef, onion, carrot, ½ can tomato sauce, egg, salt, Italian seasoning and pepper in medium bowl. Shape beef mixture into 1½-inch balls. Place meatballs in prepared pan; top with remaining ½ can tomato sauce.

3. Bake 15 to 20 minutes or until meatballs are browned and cooked through. Remove from oven; cover with foil to keep warm.

4. Open buns and arrange on baking sheet. Place 2 cheese halves on bottom of each bun. Heat buns about 7 minutes or until cheese is softened. Spoon meatballs and sauce into each bun. *Makes 6 servings*

Prep Time: 20 minutes
Cook Time: 15 minutes
Bake Time: 7 minutes

not-so-sloppy joes

super sweets
& treats

foxy face foldovers

1 ripe medium banana
1 package (17.3 ounces) frozen puff pastry sheets, thawed according
    to package directions
9 tablespoons semisweet chocolate chips, divided
36 sliced almonds
18 dried sweetened cranberries

1. Preheat oven to 400°F.

2. Peel banana and place in resealable food storage bag; seal. Knead bag to mash banana into pulp. Place puff pastry sheets on lightly floured surface; cut each sheet into 9 squares.

3. Place 9 chocolate chips (about 1 teaspoon) in center of each square. Cut small corner off one end of banana-filled bag. Squeeze small amount (about ½ teaspoon) banana pulp over chocolate chips.

4. Fold each puff pastry square diagonally in half to create triangle; press edges together with tines of fork to seal. Place pastry triangles on ungreased baking sheets.

5. Bake 14 minutes, rotating baking sheets halfway through baking time. Remove to wire racks to cool completely.

6. When pastries are cool, place remaining 6 tablespoons chocolate chips in small resealable food storage bag. Microwave on HIGH 30 seconds or until melted. Cut small corner off one end of bag; use melted chocolate to create ears and whiskers and to attach almonds and cranberries for eyes and noses.

Makes 18 pastries

foxy face foldovers

raspberry brownie pudding parfaits

1 package (6-serving size) vanilla cook-and-serve pudding and pie filling mix
½ cup white chocolate chips
1 (8-inch) prepared brownie layer
½ cup raspberry jam
1 pint fresh raspberries
Whipped topping (optional)

1. Prepare pudding according to package directions; remove from heat. Immediately stir in white chocolate chips until melted and smooth. Place pudding in small bowl. Cover and chill 2 hours.

2. Cut brownies into ½-inch cubes. Layer brownie cubes, pudding, jam and raspberries in 8 parfait glasses. Top with whipped topping.

Makes 8 servings

Tip: Homemade brownies or brownies prepared from a mix can also be used in these parfaits. Or substitute your favorite cookies, broken into chunks.

quick cookie cupcakes

1 package (about 16 ounces) refrigerated chocolate chip cookie dough (24 count)
1 cup chocolate frosting
Colored decors

1. Preheat oven to 350°F. Line 24 mini (1¾-inch) muffin cups with paper baking cups.

2. Break dough into 24 pieces along score lines. Roll each piece into ball; place in prepared muffin cups. Bake 10 to 12 minutes or until golden brown. Cool cupcakes in pans 5 minutes. Remove from pans; cool on wire racks.

3. Spread frosting over each cupcake. Sprinkle with decors.

Makes 24 mini cupcakes

raspberry brownie pudding parfaits

give me s'more muffins

    2 cups graham cracker crumbs
    ⅓ cup sugar
    ⅓ cup mini chocolate chips
    2 teaspoons baking powder
    ¾ cup milk
    1 egg
   24 milk chocolate candy kisses, unwrapped
    2 cups mini marshmallows

1. Preheat oven to 350°F. Line 24 mini (1¾-inch) muffin cups with paper baking cups.

2. Combine graham cracker crumbs, sugar, chocolate chips and baking powder in medium bowl. Whisk milk and egg in small bowl; stir into crumb mixture until well blended.

3. Spoon batter into prepared muffin cups, filling about half full. Press chocolate kiss in center of each cup. Press 4 marshmallows around each kiss.

4. Bake 10 to 12 minutes or until marshmallows are lightly browned. Cool muffins in pans 10 minutes. Remove from pans; cool completely on wire racks.   *Makes 24 mini muffins*

frozen fudge pops

    ½ cup nonfat sweetened condensed milk
    ¼ cup unsweetened cocoa powder
   1¼ cups evaporated skim milk
    1 teaspoon vanilla
    8 small paper cups and popsicle sticks

1. Beat sweetened condensed milk and cocoa in medium bowl until blended. Add evaporated milk and vanilla; beat until smooth.

2. Pour mixture into paper cups. Freeze about 2 hours or until almost firm. Insert popsicle stick into center of each cup; freeze until solid.

Makes 8 pops

give me s'more muffins

peanutty crispy dessert cups

⅓ cup creamy peanut butter

2 tablespoons butter

3 cups large marshmallows

3 cups chocolate-flavored crisp rice cereal

   Ice cream or frozen yogurt

   Assorted toppings such as chocolate sauce, sprinkles, chopped peanuts, strawberries and/or maraschino cherries

1. Heat peanut butter and butter in medium saucepan over low heat until melted and smooth. Add marshmallows; cook until melted, stirring constantly. Remove pan from heat; stir in cereal until well blended and cooled slightly.

2. Scoop mixture evenly into 12 standard (2½-inch) nonstick muffin cups; press into bottoms and up sides of cups.

3. Refrigerate 5 to 10 minutes or until set. Remove cups from pan; fill with ice cream and top with desired toppings.   *Makes 12 servings*

sparkling strawberry floats

2 tablespoons pink colored sugar (optional)

2 cups (8 ounces) frozen unsweetened strawberries

1 container (6 ounces) strawberry yogurt

½ cup milk

2 tablespoons honey or sugar

2 scoops strawberry sorbet

2 fresh strawberries (optional)

1. Place sugar in small shallow dish. Wet rims of glasses with damp paper towel; dip into sugar. Place glasses upright to dry.

2. Combine frozen strawberries, yogurt, milk and honey in blender; blend until smooth. Pour into prepared glasses; top with scoop of strawberry sorbet. Cut fresh strawberries from tip almost to stem end; place on rim of glasses.   *Makes 2 servings*

peanutty crispy dessert cups

pudding cones

1¼ cups reduced-fat (2%) milk
1 package (4-serving size) vanilla instant pudding and pie filling mix
1 cup whipped topping
½ cup chopped fruit, such as strawberries or raspberries
Uncooked rice
6 sugar cones

1. Beat milk and pudding mix with electric mixer at high speed 2 minutes or until thickened. Gently fold in whipped topping and fruit.

2. Fill medium bowl half full with rice. Fill each cone with ¼ cup pudding mixture and stand upright in rice. Place bowl in refrigerator 10 to 15 minutes or until pudding is set and slightly chilled.   *Makes 6 cones*

Variations: Substitute chopped chocolate sandwich cookies, chopped candy or candy-coated chocolates for fruit. Try different flavors of instant pudding instead of vanilla.

chocolate cereal bars

6 cups crisp rice cereal
1 jar (7 ounces) marshmallow creme
1 cup (6 ounces) semisweet chocolate chips
2 tablespoons butter or margarine
1 teaspoon vanilla

1. Grease 13×9-inch baking pan. Place cereal in large heatproof bowl.

2. Melt marshmallow creme, chocolate chips and butter in small heavy saucepan over medium heat, stirring occasionally. Remove from heat; stir in vanilla.

3. Pour chocolate mixture over cereal; stir until blended. Press into prepared pan. Cool before cutting into squares.   *Makes 24 bars*

pudding cones

cookie pizza

1 package (about 16 ounces) refrigerated sugar or peanut butter
   cookie dough
All-purpose flour (optional)
1 cup (6 ounces) semisweet chocolate chips
1 tablespoon plus 2 teaspoons shortening, divided
Candy-coated chocolate chips, mini marshmallows, roasted peanuts
   and assorted candies for toppings
¼ cup white chocolate chips

1. Preheat oven to 350°F. Generously grease 12-inch pizza pan. Let dough
stand at room temperature about 15 minutes.

2. Press dough onto prepared pan, leaving about ¾ inch between edge of
dough and pan. Sprinkle dough with flour to minimize sticking, if necessary.

3. Bake 14 to 23 minutes or until golden brown and set in center. Cool
completely in pan on wire rack. Run metal spatula between cookie and
pan after 10 to 15 minutes to loosen.

4. Combine semisweet chocolate chips and 1 tablespoon shortening in
microwavable bowl. Microwave on HIGH 1 minute; stir. Repeat process at
10- to 20-second intervals until chocolate is melted and smooth. Spread
chocolate over crust to within 1 inch of edge. Decorate with desired
toppings.

5. Combine white chocolate chips and remaining 2 teaspoons shortening in
another microwavable bowl. Microwave on MEDIUM-HIGH (70%) 1 minute;
stir. Repeat process at 10- to 20-second intervals until chocolate is melted
and smooth. Drizzle white chocolate over toppings to resemble mozzarella
cheese.   *Makes 10 to 12 servings*

cookie pizza

tea party rice pudding

3½ cups milk
⅔ cup quick-cooking rice
1 package (4-serving size) vanilla cook-and-serve pudding and pie filling mix
¼ cup sugar
¼ teaspoon ground cinnamon
¼ cup dried cherries or cranberries
¼ teaspoon vanilla extract
Additional ground cinnamon (optional)

1. Combine milk, rice, pudding mix, sugar and cinnamon in medium saucepan. Bring to a boil over medium heat, stirring occasionally. Cook and stir about 6 minutes or until thickened.

2. Remove from heat; stir in cherries and vanilla. Cool 5 minutes; spoon into 6 (6- to 8-ounce) tea cups. Serve warm, or cover surface of each cup with plastic wrap and refrigerate 1 to 2 hours. Sprinkle with additional cinnamon before serving, if desired. *Makes 6 servings*

Prep Time: 15 minutes
Chill Time: 1 hour

luau fruit cups

1 container (6 ounces) piña colada, lemon or vanilla low-fat yogurt
4 waffle cups or cones
2 cups cut-up pineapple, strawberries, mango and green grapes
Ground nutmeg
2 tablespoons flaked coconut, toasted (optional)

Spoon about 1 tablespoon yogurt into each waffle cup. Top evenly with fruit; spoon remaining yogurt over fruit. Sprinkle with nutmeg and coconut. Serve immediately. *Makes 4 servings*

tea party rice pudding

triple orange whip

1 package (3 ounces) orange gelatin
1 cup boiling water
⅔ cup orange juice
1 container (6 ounces) orange or lemon low-fat yogurt
Fresh berries and apple slices (optional)

1. Dissolve gelatin in boiling water in medium bowl. Stir in orange juice. Cover and chill about 1 hour or until partially set (consistency of unbeaten egg whites).

2. Add yogurt to gelatin mixture; beat with electric mixer at medium speed until light and fluffy. Chill until mixture thickens.

3. Spoon gelatin mixture into 4 small dessert dishes. Arrange berries and apple slices on top to create faces. *Makes 4 servings*

chunky chews

1 cup powdered sugar, divided
½ cup chunky peanut butter
2 tablespoons honey
2 tablespoons coconut, plus additional for coating
2 tablespoons raisins
2 tablespoons chopped nuts

1. Combine ½ cup powdered sugar, peanut butter and honey in medium bowl until well blended. (Mixture may be crumbly.) Add 2 tablespoons coconut and raisins; mix well. Form dough into ¾-inch balls.

2. Coat balls in remaining ½ cup powdered sugar, additional coconut and chopped nuts. Store in airtight container up to 4 days.

Makes about 3 dozen chews

triple orange whip

chocolate peanut butter candy bars

1 package (about 18 ounces) devil's food or dark chocolate cake mix *without* pudding in the mix
1 can (5 ounces) evaporated milk
⅓ cup butter, melted
½ cup dry-roasted peanuts
4 packages (1½ ounces each) chocolate peanut butter cups, coarsely chopped

1. Preheat oven to 350°F. Lightly grease 13×9-inch baking pan.

2. Beat cake mix, evaporated milk and butter in large bowl with electric mixer at medium speed until well blended. (Dough will be stiff.) Spread two thirds of dough in prepared pan. Sprinkle with peanuts.

3. Bake 10 minutes; remove from oven and sprinkle with chopped candy. Drop remaining dough by large spoonfuls over candy. Bake 15 to 20 minutes or until set. Cool completely in pan on wire rack.   *Makes 24 servings*

banana split shakes

1 small ripe banana
¼ cup fat-free (skim) milk
5 maraschino cherries, drained, plus additional for garnish
1 tablespoon light chocolate syrup
⅛ teaspoon coconut extract
4 cups low-fat chocolate frozen yogurt

1. Combine banana, milk, cherries, chocolate syrup and coconut extract in blender; blend until smooth.

2. Add yogurt, 1 cup at a time; cover and pulse after each addition until smooth and thick. Pour into 4 glasses. Garnish with additional maraschino cherries.   *Makes 4 servings*

Tip: For a low-fat shake, chop 3 large, peeled bananas. Place in resealable food storage bag and freeze until solid. (This is a great use for overripe bananas). Blend with milk, cherries, chocolate syrup and coconut extract. It will not be as thick and frosty, but will be even lower in calories and fat.

chocolate peanut butter candy bars

pretty pink pies

1 small ripe banana, sliced
1 package (4 ounces) mini graham cracker crumb pie crusts (6 crusts)
2 tablespoons chocolate ice cream topping
2 containers (6 ounces each) strawberry low-fat yogurt
6 mini pastel marshmallows
6 medium fresh strawberries, cut into wedges

1. Arrange banana slices evenly in pie crusts. Drizzle with 1 teaspoon chocolate topping; top with yogurt.

2. Place 1 marshmallow in center of each pie. Arrange strawberry wedges around marshmallow to resemble flower. Serve immediately or cover and refrigerate up to 4 hours. *Makes 6 servings*

chocolate crunchies

1 package (about 16 ounces) refrigerated sugar cookie dough
½ cup unsweetened cocoa powder
1 egg
3 bars (1.55 ounces each) milk chocolate candy with crisp rice, chopped

1. Preheat oven to 350°F. Lightly grease cookie sheets. Let dough stand at room temperature about 15 minutes.

2. Beat dough, cocoa and egg in large bowl until well blended. Stir in candy. Shape dough into ¾-inch balls; place 2 inches apart on prepared cookie sheets.

3. Bake 7 to 9 minutes or until set. Cool cookies on cookie sheets 1 minute; remove to wire racks to cool completely. *Makes about 3 dozen cookies*

pretty pink pies

secret ingredient brownies

1 cup packed brown sugar
1 cup applesauce
½ cup (1 stick) butter, melted
2 eggs
1 teaspoon vanilla
1 cup all-purpose flour
⅓ cup unsweetened cocoa powder
⅓ cup mini chocolate chips
2 teaspoons baking powder
2 teaspoons baking soda
½ teaspoon salt
½ teaspoon ground cinnamon
   Powdered sugar

1. Preheat oven to 350°F. Spray 8-inch square baking pan with nonstick cooking spray.

2. Whisk brown sugar, applesauce, butter, eggs and vanilla in large bowl until well blended. Stir in flour, cocoa, chocolate chips, baking powder, baking soda, salt and cinnamon; mix well. Pour batter into prepared pan.

3. Bake 30 to 35 minutes or until brownies begin to pull away from sides of pan and toothpick inserted into center comes out clean. Cool in pan on wire rack. Sprinkle with powdered sugar just before serving.

Makes 16 brownies

Note: Brownies will stay fresh up to 3 days. Wrap and store at room temperature.

Prep Time: 15 minutes
Bake Time: 30 minutes

acknowledgments

*The publisher would like to thank the companies and organizations
listed below for the use of their recipes and photographs
in this publication.*

Del Monte Corporation

JOLLY TIME® Pop Corn

National Watermelon Promotion Board

The Quaker® Oatmeal Kitchens

Reckitt Benckiser Inc.

Unilever

metric conversion chart

VOLUME MEASUREMENTS (dry)

1/8 teaspoon = 0.5 mL
1/4 teaspoon = 1 mL
1/2 teaspoon = 2 mL
3/4 teaspoon = 4 mL
1 teaspoon = 5 mL
1 tablespoon = 15 mL
2 tablespoons = 30 mL
1/4 cup = 60 mL
1/3 cup = 75 mL
1/2 cup = 125 mL
2/3 cup = 150 mL
3/4 cup = 175 mL
1 cup = 250 mL
2 cups = 1 pint = 500 mL
3 cups = 750 mL
4 cups = 1 quart = 1 L

VOLUME MEASUREMENTS (fluid)

1 fluid ounce (2 tablespoons) = 30 mL
4 fluid ounces (1/2 cup) = 125 mL
8 fluid ounces (1 cup) = 250 mL
12 fluid ounces (1 1/2 cups) = 375 mL
16 fluid ounces (2 cups) = 500 mL

WEIGHTS (mass)

1/2 ounce = 15 g
1 ounce = 30 g
3 ounces = 90 g
4 ounces = 120 g
8 ounces = 225 g
10 ounces = 285 g
12 ounces = 360 g
16 ounces = 1 pound = 450 g

DIMENSIONS

1/16 inch = 2 mm
1/8 inch = 3 mm
1/4 inch = 6 mm
1/2 inch = 1.5 cm
3/4 inch = 2 cm
1 inch = 2.5 cm

OVEN TEMPERATURES

250°F = 120°C
275°F = 140°C
300°F = 150°C
325°F = 160°C
350°F = 180°C
375°F = 190°C
400°F = 200°C
425°F = 220°C
450°F = 230°C

BAKING PAN SIZES

Utensil	Size in Inches/Quarts	Metric Volume	Size in Centimeters
Baking or Cake Pan (square or rectangular)	8×8×2	2 L	20×20×5
	9×9×2	2.5 L	23×23×5
	12×8×2	3 L	30×20×5
	13×9×2	3.5 L	33×23×5
Loaf Pan	8×4×3	1.5 L	20×10×7
	9×5×3	2 L	23×13×7
Round Layer Cake Pan	8×1½	1.2 L	20×4
	9×1½	1.5 L	23×4
Pie Plate	8×1¼	750 mL	20×3
	9×1¼	1 L	23×3
Baking Dish or Casserole	1 quart	1 L	—
	1½ quart	1.5 L	—
	2 quart	2 L	—